Published by Creative Education
P.O. Box 227, Mankato, Minnesota 56002
Creative Education is an imprint of
The Creative Company
www.thecreativecompany.us

Design and production by The Design Lab
Art direction by Rita Marshall
Printed by Corporate Graphics
in the United States of America

Photographs by Alamy (John Lander, Petra Wegner)
Getty Images (Theo Allofs, Altrendo Images, Darrell
Gulin, Frans Lemmens, Claus Meyer, Pete Oxford,
Joel Sartore, Craig Tuttle, Art Wolfe), iStockphoto
(Eric Isselée, Harm Kruyshaar)

Library of Congress Cataloging-in-Publication Data
Bodden, Valerie.
Parrots / by Valerie Bodden.
p. cm. — (Amazing animals)
Includes bibliographical references and index.
Summary: A basic exploration of the appearance,
behavior, and habitat of parrots, a family of colorful
birds. Also included is a story from folklore explain-
ing why parrots can imitate speech.
ISBN 978-1-58341-809-3
1. Parrots—Juvenile literature. I. Title. II. Series.
QL696.P7B63 2010
598.7'1—dc22   2009002711

CPSIA: 121510 PO1414
9 8 7 6 5 4 3

PARROTS

BY VALERIE BODDEN

CREATIVE EDUCATION

Parrots are birds. There
are more than 300 kinds of parrots in
the world. Macaws (*muh-KAHZ*) and
parakeets are kinds of parrots. So are
lorikeets and lovebirds.

Parrots live in many different parts of the world

Most parrots have colorful feathers. Parrots can be green, red, blue, or yellow. Or they can be many colors. Parrots have a strong, curved beak. They have wings for flying and strong toes to help them grab tree branches.

A parrot can have many colors on its head and face

Parrots come in many sizes.
Pygmy (*PIG-mee*) parrots are the smallest parrots. They are about as big as a sparrow. Macaws are the biggest parrots. They can be 40 inches (102 cm) long from head to tail. Some macaws weigh up to four pounds (1.8 kg).

Macaws are big birds with strong, curved beaks

Forests called rainforests, or jungles, have many parrots

Most parrots live in forests on the **continents** of South America, Africa, and Asia. Some parrots live in **deserts**. One kind of parrot even lives on snowy **mountains**!

continents Earth's seven big pieces of land

deserts big, hot areas sometimes covered with sand

mountains very big hills made of rock

Most parrots eat fruit, berries, seeds, or nuts. Some eat bugs or worms. Many parrots eat while standing on one foot. They use their other foot to hold their food.

Some kinds of parrots can use their feet like hands

Parrots are not as colorful when they are chicks

Mother parrots lay two to five eggs. When the chicks **hatch** from the eggs, most do not have any feathers. Soon, they grow feathers. The chicks learn how to fly. Small parrots can live 10 years in the wild. Big parrots can live about 50 years.

hatch come out of an egg

Parrots live together in groups called flocks. Some flocks are small. Other flocks have hundreds of birds. The birds of a flock look for food together in the morning and evening. They sleep together at night.

Parrots often group together before going to sleep

Parrots spend a lot of time cleaning their feathers. This is called preening. Parrots like to make noise, too. They can shriek, squawk, and whistle.

Parrots use their beaks to clean their feathers

Today, many people watch parrots in zoos. Other people keep parrots as pets. They even teach some kinds of parrots how to say words. These colorful birds amaze people with their beauty and brains!

Big parrots can make a lot of noise in zoos or cages

A *Parrot Story*

Why do some parrots copy what people say? People in Asia used to tell a story about this. They said that parrots used to talk on their own. Parrots always told the truth. But one day, a man tricked a parrot into lying. The people said the parrot couldn't live with them anymore. The parrot told other parrots what had happened. From then on, parrots only copied what they heard people say!

Read More

Frost, Helen. *Parrots*. Mankato, Minn.: Capstone Press, 2002.

Howard, Fran. *Parrots: Colorful Birds*. Mankato, Minn.: Capstone Press, 2005.

Web Sites

Enchanted Learning: African Gray Parrot
http://www.enchantedlearning.com/subjects/birds/printouts/Grayparrotprintout.shtml
This site has African gray parrot facts and a picture to color.

Our Animals: Parrots
http://www.abc.net.au/schoolstv/animals/PARROTS.htm
This site has parrot facts and pictures.

Index